High Voice

Daffodils, Violets & Snowflakes

24 Classical Songs for Young Women Ages Ten to Mid-Teens

Compiled by Joan Frey Boytim

T0055451

To access companion recorded piano accompaniments online, visit:
www.halleonard.com/mylibrary

Enter Code
1500-9626-7863-2689

ISBN 978-0-634-06181-3

HAL•LEONARD® CORPORATION
7777 W. Bluemound Rd. P.O. Box 13819 Milwaukee, WI 53213

In Australia Contact:
Hal Leonard Australia Pty. Ltd.
4 Lentara Court
Cheltenham, Victoria, 3192 Australia
Email: ausadmin@halleonard.com.au

For all works contained herein:
Unauthorized copying, arranging, adapting, recording, Internet posting, public performance, or other distribution of the printed or recorded music in this publication is an infringement of copyright. Infringers are liable under the law.

Visit Hal Leonard Online at
www.halleonard.com

PREFACE

Daffodils, Violets & Snowflakes is a supplementary classical solo book compiled for the enjoyment of late elementary, junior high and middle school girls. The high and low volumes each contain the same twenty-four songs, with companion accompaniments recorded by Laura Ward for those who use these learning aids.

This book is not intended to be the primary "first" book of songs; however, it can complement the *36 Solos for Young Singers* and the *Easy Songs for the Beginning Soprano* and *Easy Songs for the Beginning Mezzo-Soprano/Alto.* The songs are mostly previously out of print material which is unfamiliar but is suitable for the student with an imaginative mind and a flair for storytelling in songs such as "Daddy's Sweetheart," "Four and Twenty Snowflakes," and "Ho! Mr. Piper." Some of the songs are particularly good for playing different characters in a singing dialogue, such as "The Leaves and the Wind," "Nursery Rhymes," "To My First Love," and "You'd Better Ask Me." As the book title suggests, most of the songs relate to subjects of nature, love, flowers, birds, or the seasons.

Even though there are some short, very easy songs, there are quite a number of challenging selections for the musically talented and ambitious girls in your studio. Some of the ranges are a bit extended, but include optional notes for those students who require a limited range. Several of the songs introduce the florid style of singing with short, gentle moving passages. Many of the songs could be termed "encore" style songs, having a humorous touch to them.

In addition, women looking for solo pieces that would be particularly attractive to selected audiences, especially of young people, may find that there are many possibilities for grouping three or four songs together as "theme" sets for performance purposes.

The main intent is to provide a collection of songs that are fun to sing and still have a musicianship development component.

Joan Frey Boytim
May, 2003

CONTENTS

11	AN APRIL GIRL	J. Remington Fairlamb
4	BOATS OF MINE	Anne Stratton Miller
8	CARE FLIES FROM THE LAD THAT IS MERRY	Michael Arne
12	DADDY'S SWEETHEART	Liza Lehmann
20	DOES HE LOVE ME, OR LOVE ME NOT?	Andrew Sterling
24	THE FAIRY PIPERS	A. Herbert Brewer
30	FOUR AND TWENTY SNOWFLAKES	William Stickles
34	HEIGH-HO! THE SUNSHINE	Montague F. Phillips
38	HER DREAM	Frank Waller
40	HO! MR. PIPER	Pearl G. Curran
44	KITTY OF COLERAINE	Arr. Joan Frey Boytim
46	THE LEAVES AND THE WIND	Franco Leoni
17	THE LINNET'S SECRET	Alec Rowley
50	LITTLE MAID OF ARCADEE	Arthur Sullivan
58	THE MINUET	Joseph Mosenthal
53	MOLLY MALONE	Irish Folksong
60	MY DAFFODILS	W. Berwald
63	NURSERY RHYMES	Pearl G. Curran
70	THE SECRET	Oley Speaks
76	'TIS SPRING	Harriet Ware
73	TO MY FIRST LOVE	Hermann Löhr
88	VIOLETS	R. Huntington Woodman
80	THE WIND	Charles Gilbert Spross
84	YOU'D BETTER ASK ME	Hermann Löhr

BOATS OF MINE

Robert Louis Stevenson

Anne Stratton Miller

Copyright © 2003 by HAL LEONARD CORPORATION
International Copyright Secured All Rights Reserved

Green leaves a - float - ing,
Cas - tles of the foam, Boats of mine a -
boat - ing, When will all come home?
rit.
p a tempo

mf
accel.
On goes the riv - er And out past the
mf
accel.
dim. a tempo
mill, A - way down the val - ley, A -
dim. a tempo
way down the hill.
p
A - way down the riv - er, A
poco rit.
a tempo

hun - dred miles or more, Oth - er lit - tle
f
chil - dren Shall bring my boats a - shore,
mf
opt.
mf
poco accel.
p
Shall bring my boats a shore.
pp
p
a tempo e dim.
p
pp
a tempo
rit.
pp

CARE FLIES FROM THE LAD THAT IS MERRY

Garrick's Cymon

Michael Arne
Realization by Percy E. Fletcher

Copyright © 2003 by HAL LEONARD CORPORATION
International Copyright Secured All Rights Reserved

f
round and as red as a cher - ry.
3
f
mf
Care flies from the lad that is mer - ry,
mf
mp
Care flies from the lad that is mer - ry,
f
mp
mf
Care flies from the lad that is mer - ry, Whose
cresc.
mf

heart is as sound and cheeks are as round, As round and as
red, as red as a cher - ry, Whose
cresc.
heart is as sound and cheeks are as round, As round and as red as a
cresc.
f
cher - ry.
3

AN APRIL GIRL

Mary Mapes Dodge

J. Remington Fairlamb

* a speck in the air that is visible in sun ray

Copyright © 2003 by HAL LEONARD CORPORATION
International Copyright Secured All Rights Reserved

DADDY'S SWEETHEART

Curtis Hardin-Burnley
(Adapted)

Liza Lehmann

Copyright © 2003 by HAL LEONARD CORPORATION
International Copyright Secured All Rights Reserved

said I'd have to mar - ry a man Or be a cross old
maid. I'm so wor - ried, I don't know what to do; For
p
poco rall.
I've a se - cret, I'll tell it to you: I don't love a - ny man but my
pp
a tempo
poco rall.
colla voce
pp
a tempo
Dad - dy, And he's al - rea - dy mar - ried, don't you see?

Oh, if moth - er had - n't mar - ried Dad - dy, Dad - dy might have mar - ried
me!
p con tenerezza
Of - ten he calls me his
p dolce
cresc.
"Sweet - heart," He loves me such a lot! If

mo - ther had - n't snapp'd him up, I might have caught him, why
cresc.
Do not drag.
not? She might have cho - sen some - one else, For
opt.
ev - 'ry - bo - dy loves her, but as for my - self;
p
rall.
p
colla voce
pp a tempo
No - bo - dy loves me but my Dad - dy, And
pp a tempo

he's al - rea - dy mar - ried, don't you see?
Oh, if moth - er
had - n't mar - ried Dad - dy,
Dad - dy might have wait - ed for
sempre cresc.
rall.
pp
me!
Ah! if moth - er
had - n't mar - ried Dad - dy,
rall.
sempre cresc.
a tempo
Dad - dy might have mar - ried
me!
8va
a tempo

THE LINNET'S SECRET

Dorothy Cook

Alec Rowley

Copyright © 2003 by HAL LEONARD CORPORATION
International Copyright Secured All Rights Reserved

told it to the Breeze, Who told the Lin - net's se - cret to the
Star - lings in the trees.
Ped.
p
The Star - lings told a Wea - zel, and the
p
Wea - zel went to see What the se - cret that was hid - den 'neath the

broom could be.
But he
pp rit.
a tempo
Ped.
on - ly found an emp - ty nest, be - cause I'm glad to say,
The
mp
Lin - net's lit - tle se - crets had that morn - ing flown a - way.
mf
mf
senza rit.
with Ped.
pp
Ped.

DOES HE LOVE ME, OR LOVE ME NOT?

Music and Words by
ANDREW STERLING

Copyright © 2003 by HAL LEONARD MUSIC CORPORATION
International Copyright Secured All Rights Reserved

she had oft' heard told of a nov - el way That a
But she missed her count e'er she'd well be - gun. 'Till of
flow'r could tell if her love were true. A
leaf - lets white there re - mained no more, She
dai - sy she culled with eag - er hands: "Come
won - der'd why dark fate should hide From
whis - per" she said, "I pray, Will his
her what the dai - sy knew. Did the

heart faith - ful be? Does he sigh for me? Or, re - joice that I'm far a -
flow'r blush to tell what it knew so well That she wor - ship'd a love un -

REFRAIN
molto espressivo
way?"
true?
"Does he love me or love me not?
mf

Tell me, O sim - ple flow'r,
Has his heart all its

vows for - got? Tho' I think of him ev' - ry hour?

Is he true, as he said he'd be? Will
glad - ness soon be my lot? Give me your
an - swer, 'tis all to me, Does he love me, or love me
1
D.C.
2
not?" love opt. me not?"
D.C.

THE FAIRY PIPERS

Fred E. Weatherly

A. Herbert Brewer

Copyright © 2003 by HAL LEONARD CORPORATION
International Copyright Secured All Rights Reserved

pp
Come out! come out! Lis - ten on the air!
(8)
pp
sempre p
Up there! down there! Play - ing ev - 'ry - where! Oh hark! Oh
(8)
strict time
hear! Don't you hear the tune? Air - y fair - y pip - ers un - der -
(8)
neath the mer - ry moon!
(8)
p cresc.
dim.
pp

p
They'll play to you of Cu - pid's tricks, Of love - ly queens and
poco cresc.
kings, Of fights and fun and pol - i - tics And lots of oth - er
poco cresc.
things.
mp
cresc.
dim.
pp
Oh hark! Oh hear! Can't you hear them
pp

play? Up there! down there! Till the break of day! Oh
sempre pp
hark! Oh hear! Don't you love the tune?
strict time
Air - y fair - y
sempre pp
pip - ers un - der - neath the sil - ver moon!
p
cresc.
dim.
poco rit.
mp
Meno mosso
But if you doubt that this can be, And
pp
poco rit.
p

poco rit.
cresc.
rall.
ques - tion what I say, You'll nev - er hear the mel - o - dy The
poco rit.
cresc.
rall.
Tempo I
fair - y pip - ers play.
8va
p
a tempo
cresc.
p
Then come! come out! Lis - ten while you
(8)
dim.
pp
can, Up there! down there! Since the world be -
(8)

sempre p
gan. Oh hark! Oh hear! Oh the hap - py
(8)
Strict time
tune! Air - y fair - y pip - ers un - der -
(8)
neath the sil - ver moon!
(8)
ppp sotto voce
Come! Come!
8va
ppp

FOUR AND TWENTY SNOWFLAKES

Music and Words by
William Stickles

Copyright © 2003 by HAL LEONARD CORPORATION
International Copyright Secured All Rights Reserved

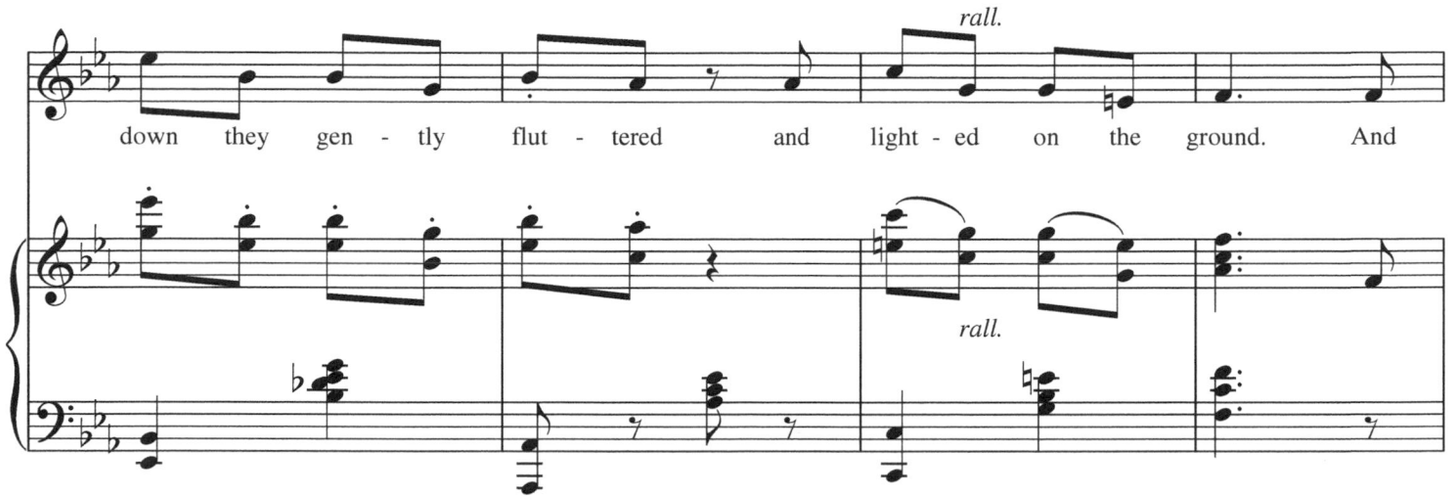
rall.
down they gen - tly flut - tered and light - ed on the ground. And
rall.

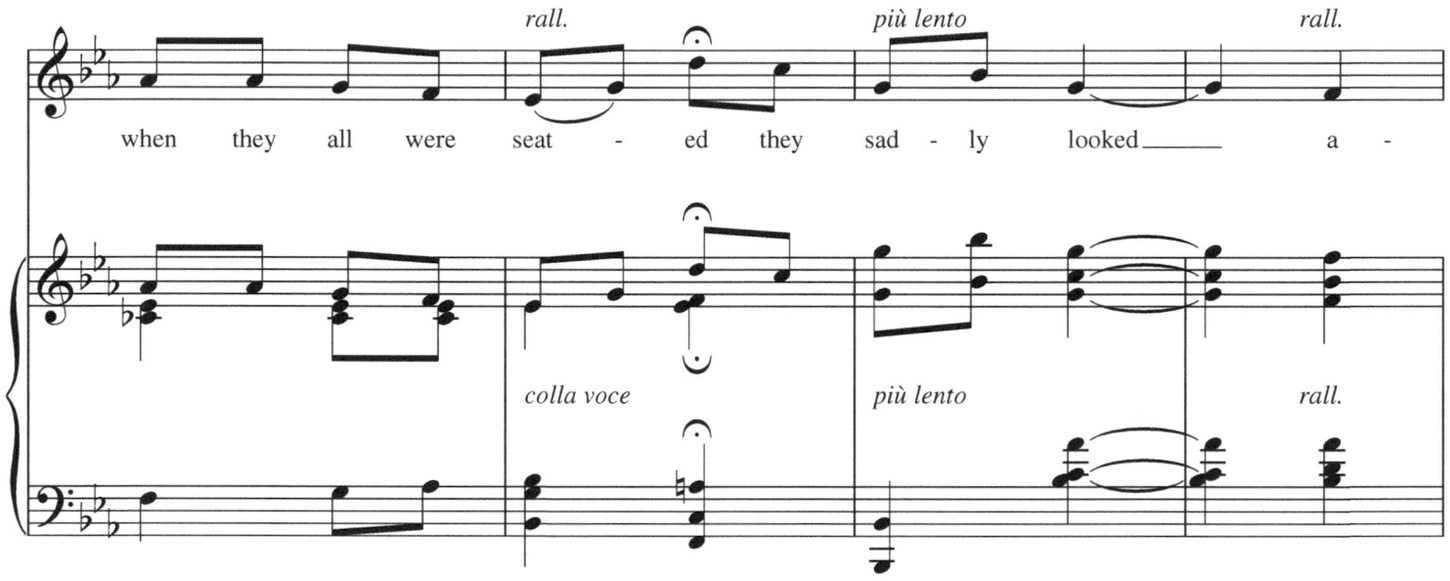
rall.
più lento
rall.
when they all were seat - ed they sad - ly looked a -
colla voce
più lento
rall.

Allegretto
round.
rall.

"We're ver - y few, in - deed," sighed they, "and we
a tempo
some - times make mis - takes, We can - not make a
rall.
a tempo
snow - drift with four and twen - ty flakes." Just
rall.
a tempo

then the sun peeped 'round a cloud and smiled at the ar -
più lento
ray And the dis - ap - point - ed snow - flakes, melt - ed
più lento
dim. e rall.
opt.
qui - et - ly a - way!
dim. e rall.

HEIGH-HO! THE SUNSHINE

Ancie B. Marsland

Montague F. Phillips

Copyright © 2003 by HAL LEONARD CORPORATION
International Copyright Secured All Rights Reserved

All thy days of lone - ly pain Go, when love comes
Ped. simile
back a - gain. Smile, and sing my glad re - frain
cresc.
Ped.
f
Heigh - ho! Heigh - ho! the sun -
ten. poco rit.
f marcato
ten.
poco rit. f
ten.
Ped.
Ped.

shine.
f
a tempo
Ped.
mf
Heigh - ho! dance and sing, Wed - ding bells shall
mf
8va
marc.
(senza Ped.)
ten.
sure - ly ring: Love's re - turn will be ere long,
ten.
ten.
simile

Shed - ding tears is sure - ly wrong. Laugh, and join my
cresc.
mer - ry song Heigh - ho! Heigh - ho! the sun -
f
opt.
ff
ten.
rit.
f marc.
rit. ff
ten.
shine.
a tempo
marc.
sf
sf
Ped.

HER DREAM

Walter S. Poague

Frank Waller

Copyright © 2003 by HAL LEONARD CORPORATION
International Copyright Secured All Rights Reserved

poco accel.
poco
I be - lieve in you." He up and kissed her then, For
poco accel.
poco

stentato
that's the way with men, And she just mur - mured
stentato
mp

ten. ad lib.
"Ah, let me dream a - gain."
m.s.
p
armonioso
colla voce
a tempo
3
mf

HO! MR. PIPER

Music and Words by
Pearl G. Curran

Copyright © 2003 by HAL LEONARD CORPORATION
International Copyright Secured All Rights Reserved

poco rit.
f
a tempo
such a sight to see!
Ho! Mis - ter Pi - per, come and play for me!
poco rit.
f
a tempo
Valzer lento
p
mf
f accel.
a tempo
Ped.
Ped.
Ped.
Ped.
Tempo I°
mf
Now I see the fair - ies com - ing,
Here they are at last!
(the Piper plays)
mf
(with enthusiasm)
Is - n't it just lots of fun To see them skip-ping past?
One has fall - en o - ver, He was
tr
f
mf

poco rit.
opt.
run - ning far too fast!
a tempo
Ah!
Ha!
poco rit.
ff
Ped. *
a tempo
Ha!!
ten.
tr
f
(with surprise)
O! Mis - ter Pi - per, I
rit.
did - n't think they'd hear:
ff
p
p colla voce
(with regret)
All the dain - ty lit - tle things be - gin to dis - ap - pear;

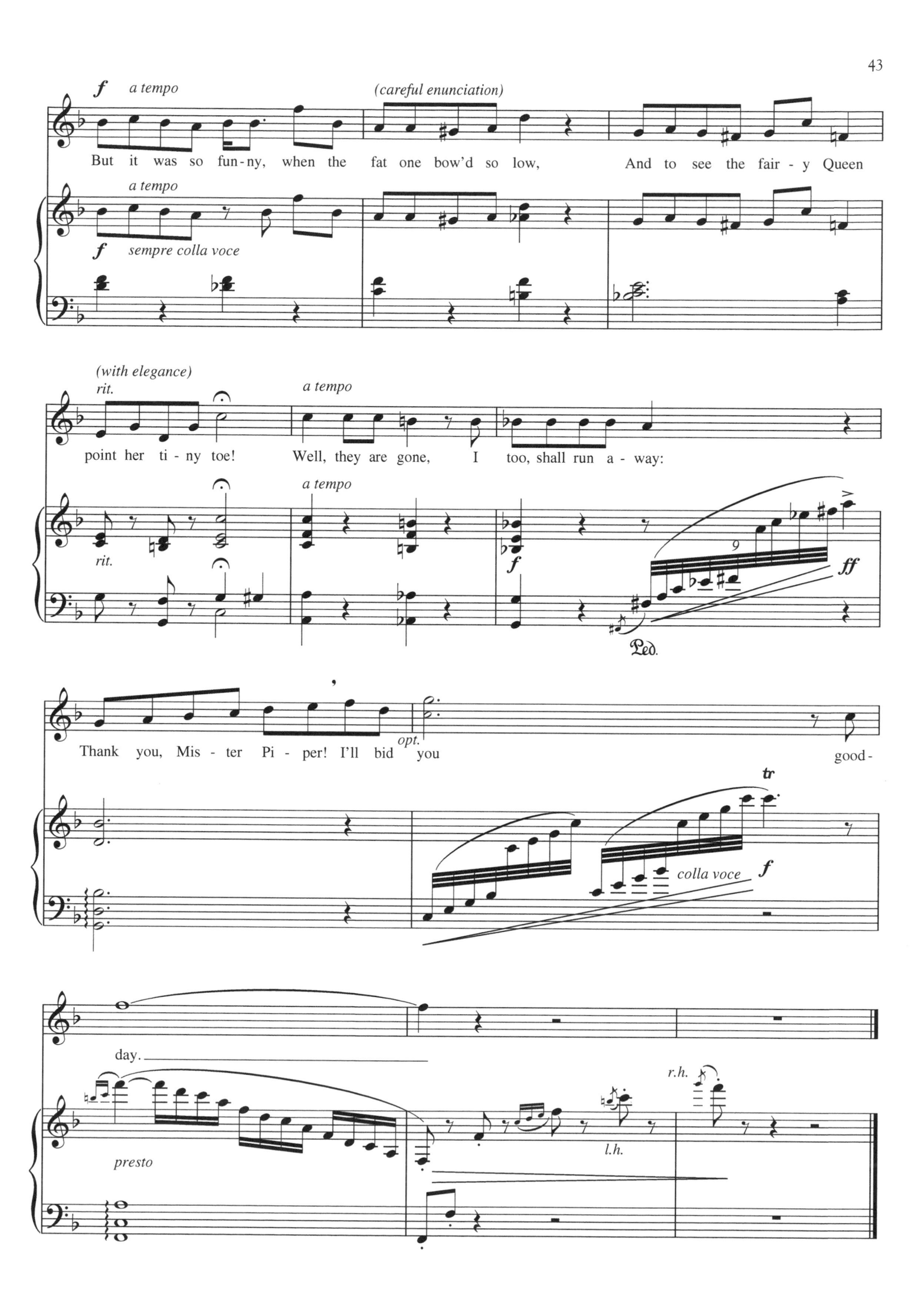
f a tempo
(careful enunciation)
But it was so fun-ny, when the fat one bow'd so low, And to see the fair - y Queen
a tempo
f sempre colla voce
(with elegance)
rit.
a tempo
point her ti - ny toe! Well, they are gone, I too, shall run a - way:
rit.
a tempo
f
ff
Ped.
Thank you, Mis - ter Pi - per! I'll bid you good-
opt.
tr
colla voce
f
day.
presto
r.h.
l.h.

KITTY OF COLERAINE

Irish Folksong
Arr. Joan Frey Boytim

Copyright © 2003 by HAL LEONARD CORPORATION
International Copyright Secured All Rights Reserved

pitch - er it tum - bled, And all the sweet but - ter - milk wat - er'd the plain. "Oh!
ere I did lave her She vow'd for such pleas - ure she'd break it a - gain. 'Twas
what shall I do now? 'Twas look - ing at you, now; Sure, sure, such a pitch - er I'll
hay - mak - ing sea - son, I can't tell the rea - son Mis - for - tune will nev - er come
ne'er meet a - gain; 'Twas the pride of my dai - ry, Oh! Bar - ney Mc - Clea - ry, You're
sin - gle, 'tis plain, For ver - y soon af - ter poor Kit - ty's dis - ast - er There
sent as a plague to the girls of Cole - raine."
was not a pitch - er found whole in Cole - raine.

THE LEAVES AND THE WIND

George Cooper

Franco Leoni

Copyright © 2003 by HAL LEONARD CORPORATION
International Copyright Secured All Rights Reserved

rit.
red and gold, Sum - mer is gone, and the days grow cold."
rit.
a tempo
Soon as the leaves heard the wind's loud call, Down they came flut - ter - ing
a tempo
mf
rit.
one and all; O - ver the brown fields they
mf
rit.
p
ten.
a tempo
danc'd and flew, Sing - ing the
p
pp

soft lit - tle songs they knew.
a tempo
mf
3
3
"Crick - et, good - bye, we've been friends so long! Lit - tle brook, sing us your fare - well song!
p
rit.
a tempo
Say you are sor - ry to see us go; Ah! you will miss us, right well we know. Dear lit - tle lambs, in your
rit.
a tempo

mf
rit.
flee - cy fold, Moth - er will keep you from harm and cold; Fond - ly we've watch'd you in vale and glade,
mf
rit.
p ten. a tempo
Say, will you dream of our lov - ing shade?" Danc - ing and whirl - ing the lit - tle leaves went, Win - ter had
pp col canto
a tempo
dim.
rit. e dim.
almost whispered
call'd them and they were con - tent. Soon fast a - sleep in their earth - y beds, The snow laid a cov-er-let o - ver their
dim.
rit. e dim.
heads.
ppp a tempo
Ped.

LITTLE MAID OF ARCADEE

from *Thespis*

W.S. Gilbert

Arthur Sullivan

Copyright © 2003 by HAL LEONARD CORPORATION
International Copyright Secured All Rights Reserved

rall.
Hap - py lit - tle maid - en she, Hap-py maid of Ar - ca - dee! Hap-py maid of Ar - ca - dee!
rall.
colla voce
cresc.
Mo - ments sped as mo - ments will, Rap - id - ly e -
nough; un - til Af - ter, say, a month or two, Rob-in did as Rob - ins do,
p
f
Fick-le as the month of May, Jilt - ed her and ran a - way!
f
rall. e dim.
Wretch-ed lit - tle maid - en she! Dole-ful maid of Ar - ca - dee! Dole - ful maid of Ar - ca - dee!
rall. e dim.

p
To her lit - tle home she crept, There she sat her down and wept;
p
riten.
Maid - en wept as maid - ens will, Grew so thin and pale and ill,
riten.
a tempo
cresc.
Till an - oth - er came to woo, Then a - gain the ros - es grew.
a tempo
cresc.
colla voce
f animato
cresc.
Hap - py lit - tle maid - en she! Hap - py maid of Ar - ca - dee!
f
cresc.
rall.
f
Hap - py lit - tle maid - en she! Hap - py maid of Ar - ca - dee! Hap - py maid of Ar - ca - dee!
rall.
f colla voce

MOLLY MALONE

Irish Folksong
Arr. by W. Rhys-Herbert

Copyright © 2003 by HAL LEONARD CORPORATION
International Copyright Secured All Rights Reserved

f a tempo
live all a - live! A - live, a - live - o! A - live a - live - o! Cry - ing
mf alla harpa

rit.
"Cock - les and mus - sels, a - live, all a - live!"
rit.
a tempo
mf

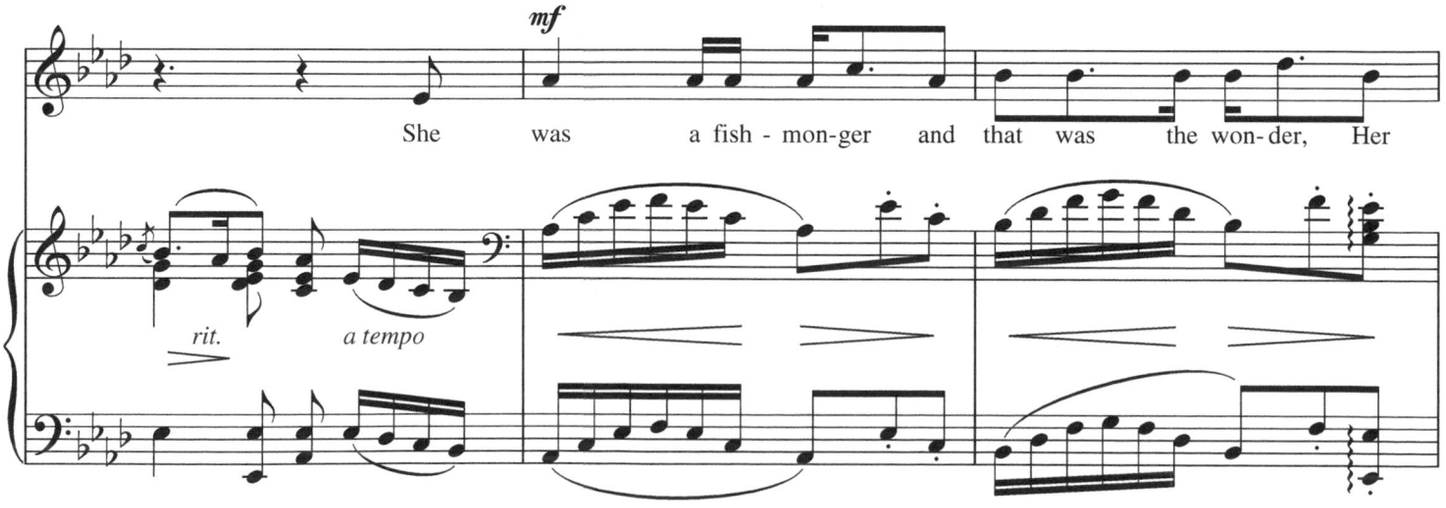
mf
She was a fish - mon-ger and that was the won-der, Her
rit.
a tempo

fa - ther and moth - er were fish mon - gers too, They
drove wheel - bar - rows thro' streets broad and nar - row, Cry - ing
rit.
f
"Cock - les and mus - sels, a - live all a - live!" A -
colla voce
rit.
mf

a tempo
live, a - live - o! A - live, a - live - o! Cry - ing
alla harpa
rit.
"Cock - les and mus - sels, a - live all a - live!"
rit.
She
Slower
pp Much slower
died of the fa - vor,* and noth - ing could save her, And
pp Much slower

*fever

that was the end of sweet Mol - ly Ma - lone, But her
ghost drives a bar - row thro' streets broad and nar - row, Cry - ing
pp
"Cock - les and mus - sels a - live all a - live!"
p a tempo
A - live, a - live - o! A -
pp alla harpa
live, a - live - o! Cry - ing "Cock - les and mus - sels, a - live all a - live!"
rit.
rit.

THE MINUET

Mary Mapes Dodge

Joseph Mosenthal

Copyright © 2003 by HAL LEONARD CORPORATION
International Copyright Secured All Rights Reserved

p
go, Long a - go. How she held her pret - ty head, How her
go, Long a - go. Bless her! why, she wears a cap, Grand - ma
go, Long a - go. Brave but mod - est, grand - ly shy She would
p
cresc.
dain - ty skirt she spread, Turn - ing out her lit - tle toes; How she
does, and takes a nap Ev - 'ry sin - gle day; and yet Grand - ma
like to have us try Just to feel like those who met In the
cresc.
f
slow - ly leaned and rose Long a - go,
danced the min - u - et Long a - go,
grace - ful min - u - et Long a - go,
f
Long a - go.
Long a - go.
Long a - go.
f

MY DAFFODILS

Fred G. Bowles

W. Berwald

Copyright © 2003 by HAL LEONARD CORPORATION
International Copyright Secured All Rights Reserved

ten.
poco rall.
shine as in those days of old. But O, my heart is fair to be Where
ten.
poco rall.
mp a tempo
all my daf - fo - dils are free. My heart is with the daf - fo - dils, By
a tempo
mp
cresc.
flow - ing rills, by laugh - ing hills; Their gold - en mu - sic seems to blow Wher -
cresc.
f
ev - er light and laugh - ter go.
And
f
accel. e giocoso
dim.
p

pp
un poco rallentare
ten.
ten.
once a - gain, as in a dream, My thoughts go fly - ing to a stream Where
un poco rallentare
ten.
ten.
pp
pp
daf - fo - dil and daf - fo - dil With gold - en col - or soft - ly fill
poco accel.
f
largando
A val - ley set be - neath the hills, O daf - fo - dils! my daf - fo - dils!
poco accel.
largando
f
mp
f
O daf-fo- dils! my daf - - - fo - dils!
a tempo
8va
accel.
f
Ped.

NURSERY RHYMES

Music and Words by
Pearl G. Curran

Copyright © 2003 by HAL LEONARD CORPORATION
International Copyright Secured All Rights Reserved

Hey! did - dle did - dle, The cat and the fid - dle, And the cow jump - ing ov - er the
Ped.
moon; How the lit - tle dog laugh'd with glee, He had
l.h.
p
Ped.
nev - er seen such sport, you see. And now, as I re - call, That
real - ly was - n't all, For the dish ran a - way with the spoon! The
Ped.

dish ran a - way with the spoon!
Ped.
Ped.
accel. molto
mf
And old Moth - er Hub - bard, She went to the cup - board, To
a tempo
f
mf
get her poor dog a bone; But when she got there The
patetico
f
cup - board was bare, And so the poor dog - gie had none. And
colla voce

Vivace
riten.
Hump - ty Dump - ty sat on a wall, and Hump - ty Dump - ty had a great fall,
f
colla voce
fz
Ped.
8vb
a tempo
mf
declamato
And all the King's hors - es and
ff
precipitato
mf
allarg.
all the King's men, and all the King's hor - ses and all the King's men
colla voce
a tempo
mf
Could - n't put Hump - ty to - geth - er
a -
fz
precipitato
dim.
mf

Marcia funebre
Allegro
opt. ten.
ten.
gain.
But Old King Cole was a mer - ry old soul, A
mer - ry old soul was he; He called for his pipe, and he called for his bowl, And he
called for his Fid - dlers Three. And ev - 'ry Fid - dler had a fine fid - dle, A ver - y fine fid - dle had
l.h.
he.
Twee - dle - dee!
Twee - dle -

Tempo Iº
f
dee! Twee-dle - dee! went the Fid - dlers Three!
f
Ped.
poco rit.
Ped.
Ped.
p
Lit - tle girl - ie with your hair of gold, Moth - er Goose Rhymes I've
a tempo
p
poco a poco rall.
told; But I see the Sand - man com - ing, and sleep - y tunes he's hum - ming, So I'll
poco a poco rall.

Andante
tuck you in from the cold, And we'll sing a lit - tle lul - la - by:
l.h.
Bye - low, Ba - by - Bye, Yes, I know a lot more Rhymes That we'll
pp
keep for oth - er times, And we'll take a lit - tle nap, you and I, We'll
Ped.
rall.
take a lit - tle nap, you and I.
rallent.
morendo
Ped.
Ped.

THE SECRET

Music and Words by
Oley Speaks

Copyright © 2003 by HAL LEONARD CORPORATION
International Copyright Secured All Rights Reserved

f
mf
dew;
The
f
senza rit.
dew - drop told the rob - in, (who nev - er could keep a
mf
capriccioso e leggiero
mp
thing!) He perched all day on a
p
blos - som - ing spray, he perched all day on a

cresc.
blos - som - ing spray, he perched all day on a blos - som - ing
cresc.
f
accel.
ten.
ff
spray, And war - bled: "It's spring, it's spring, it's spring!" And
f
accel.
ten.
ff
rit.
fff
war - bled: "It's spring, it's spring!"
rit.
fff
molto vivace
Ped.
8va

TO MY FIRST LOVE

Edwin Hamilton

Hermann Löhr

Copyright © 2003 by HAL LEONARD CORPORATION
International Copyright Secured All Rights Reserved

sode) I was gush - ing you were shy, You were blush - ing, so was
rall.
I. I was smit - ten, ve - ry true; Bad - ly bit - ten, so were you.
rall.
mf
p
A - ny mon - ey? not a
p
bit; Rath - er fun - ny, was - n't it? Vows we plight - ed, hap - py pair! How de - light - ed peo - ple

were! But your fa - ther, to be sure, Thought it ra - ther pre - ma -
cresc.
ture; And your moth - er, strange to say, Was an - oth - er in the
cresc.
f
rall.
p
way. What a heav - en van - ished then! (You were sev - en, I was ten.) That was ma - ny years a -
f
p colla voce
pp
go; Don't let a - ny - bo - dy know!
colla voce

'TIS SPRING

Montrose J. Moses

Harriet Ware

Copyright © 2003 by HAL LEONARD CORPORATION
International Copyright Secured All Rights Reserved

rit.
air with its May - time, The heart in its
rit.
a tempo
play - time, The blue in the sky.
a tempo
pp
tr
The

cresc.
rob - ins are sing - ing, The blue - birds are wing - ing, The blos - soms are
8va
p
cling - ing, On vine and on tree; And hey! for the sun now, And
(8)
rit.
hey! for the fun now, And all to be done now, By you and by
(8)
rit.
a tempo
me.
Broader
f
Then ho! for the
a tempo
f
Ped.

show - ers, The fruit and the flow - ers, The bright sun - ny hours, The
lark's on the wing; A - way we will go now, The boughs are bent
rit.
low now, And life's in a glow now, 'Tis Spring, ah! 'Tis Spring!
rit.
accel. cresc.
Ped.
Ped.
8va

THE WIND

Carolyn S. Bailey

Charles Gilbert Spross

Copyright © 2003 by HAL LEONARD CORPORATION
International Copyright Secured All Rights Reserved

a tempo
p
so. The lit - tle brown hare for - got to run, The blue - jay for - got to
p
a tempo
f
rall.
a tempo
fly; And the lit - tle brown seeds That spring - time needs, Cried, "When will the Wind come
f
rall.
a tempo
molto meno mosso
p
by, When will the Wind come by?" The
f
rall.
p
molto meno mosso

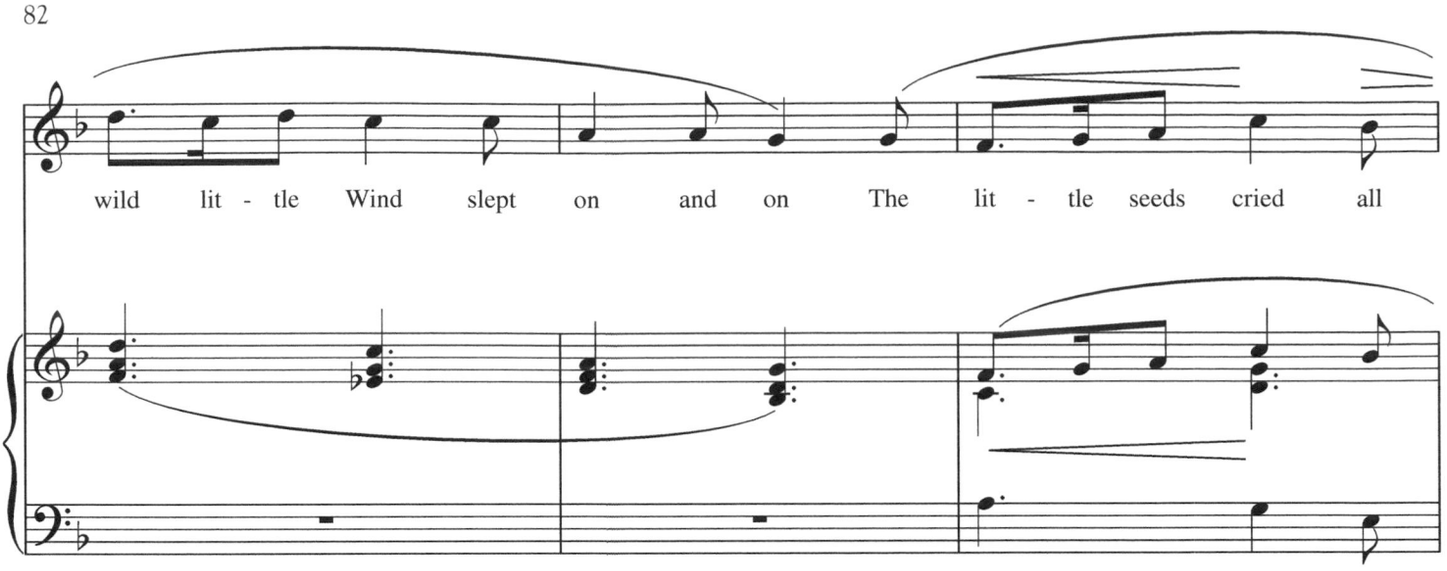
wild lit - tle Wind slept on and on The lit - tle seeds cried all

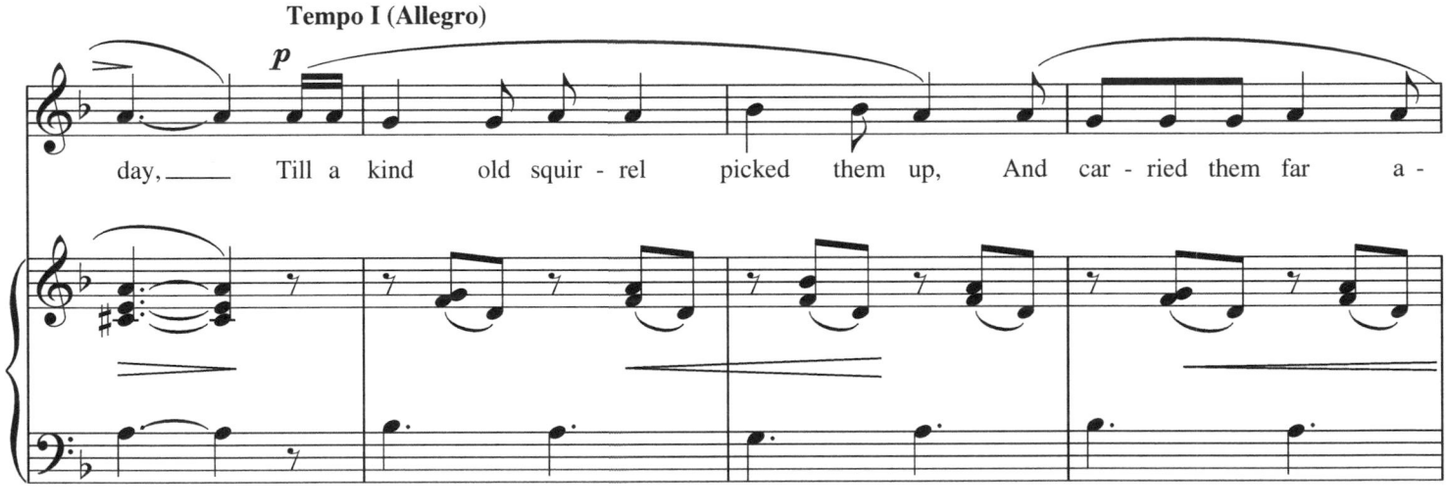
Tempo I (Allegro)
p
day, Till a kind old squir - rel picked them up, And car - ried them far a -

rall.
way To the place where lit - tle seeds want to go, And he plant-ed them ev - 'ry
rall.

a tempo
one So the wild lit - tle Wind woke up to find That all of his work was
a tempo
f
done, That all of his work was done.
opt.
Vivace
8va
f
ff
8va
f

YOU'D BETTER ASK ME

Samuel Lover

Hermann Löhr

Copyright © 2003 by HAL LEONARD CORPORATION
International Copyright Secured All Rights Reserved

f
ceiv - ers, And nev - er, I know will con - sent. She says, girls in a hur - ry who
f
mar - ry, At lei - sure re - pent."
colla voce
p
mf
Then sup - pose I would talk to your fa - ther, sweet Ma - ry, says I. "Oh! don't
talk to my fa - ther, says Ma - ry, be - gin - ning to cry; For my fa-ther he loves me so

f
dear - ly, He'll nev - er con - sent I should go. If you
talk to my fa - ther, says Ma - ry, He'll sure - ly say,
f
colla voce
"No!"
p
Then
how shall I get you, my jew - el, sweet Ma - ry? says I. If your
p

fa - ther and moth - er's so cru - el, most sure - ly I'll die.
mf
"Oh! nev - er say die, dear," says Ma - ry, "A
way now to save you I see, Since my pa - rents are both so con - tra - ry,
f
f rall.
You'd bet - ter ask me!"
rall.
a tempo

VIOLETS

Music and Words by
R. Huntington Woodman

Copyright © 2003 by HAL LEONARD CORPORATION
International Copyright Secured All Rights Reserved